The TINY TITANOSAURS

Luis Chiappe's Dinosaur Nests

by Natalie Lunis

Consultant: Dr. Luis M. Chiappe, Director
The Dinosaur Institute
Natural History Museum of Los Angeles County

BEARPORT
PUBLISHING

New York, New York

Credits

Cover, © L. Chiappe; Title Page, © L. Chiappe; 4, © L. Chiappe; 5, © L. Chiappe; 6L, © L. Chiappe; 6R, Kathrin Ayer; 7, © L. Chiappe; 8, © L. Chiappe; 9, © L. Chiappe; 11, © L. Chiappe; 12L, © Laurie O'Keefe/Photo Researchers, Inc.; 12R, © Publiphoto/Photo Researchers, Inc.; 13T, © Joe Tucciarone/ Photo Researchers, Inc.; 13B, © Jon Hughes/Bedrock Studios/Dorling Kindersley; 14, © Louie Psihoyos/Science Faction.net; 15, © L. Chiappe; 16T, © L. Chiappe; 16B, © K.Meeker/L. Chiappe; 17, © R. Meier/L. Chiappe; 18T, © L. Chiappe; 18B, © L. Chiappe; 19, © Mick Ellison/National Geographic; 20L, © MCA/Universal Pictures/Photofest; 20R, © MCA/Universal Pictures/Photofest; 21, © Universal Pictures/Photofest; 22, © Robert Clark; 23, © R. Meier/L. Chiappe; 24, Kathrin Ayer; 25, © R. Meier/L. Chiappe; 26L, © Mick Ellison; 26R, © L. Chiappe; 27, © L. Chiappe; 28–29, Rodica Prato; 28, © Natural History Museum, England; 29T, Kathrin Ayer; 29B, Kathrin Ayer.

Publisher: Kenn Goin
Editorial Director: Adam Siegel
Creative Director: Spencer Brinker
Photo Researcher: Beaura Kathy Ringrose
Design: Dawn Beard Creative

Library of Congress Cataloging-in-Publication Data
Lunis, Natalie.
The tiny Titanosaurs : Luis Chiappe's dinosaur nests / by Natalie Lunis.
    p. cm. — (Fossil hunters)
Includes bibliographical references and index.
ISBN-13: 978-1-59716-373-6 (library binding)
ISBN-10: 1-59716-373-2 (library binding)
1. Titanosaurus—Juvenile literature. I. Title.

QE862.S3.L86 2007
567.913—dc22

                          2006034397

For more information, write to Bearport Publishing Company, Inc., 101 Fifth Avenue, Suite 6R, New York, New York 10003. Printed in the United States of America.

10 9 8 7 6 5 4 3 2 1

Table of Contents

A Lucky Day

Luis Chiappe (*kee*-AH-pay) did not take his eyes off the ground. He and his team had come to the **badlands** of Patagonia (*pat*-uh-GOH-nee-uh) in search of **fossils**. Now they walked back and forth, scanning the dry, rocky earth for scraps of **ancient** bone.

Luis Chiappe

Patagonia is a huge area in South America. It is larger than Texas and Oklahoma put together. Most of Patagonia is in Argentina. A small part is in Chile (CHIL-ay).

Like all good fossil hunters, the team knew that one small piece of bone is often a clue that more bones are buried nearby. On a lucky day, one piece might even lead to a huge skeleton or other rare fossil.

Today would turn out to be very, very lucky. The team was about to find lots of fossils—but not the kind that they expected.

The badlands where the team searched are dry and dusty and surrounded by low hills.

Searching for Early Birds

Luis Chiappe was a **paleontologist** working at the American Museum of Natural History in New York City. Yet he knew the badlands well.

Luis was born in Argentina. He had studied with some of the country's leading scientists. He often went with them on **expeditions** to Patagonia. There, they hunted for the bones of dinosaurs, ancient birds, turtles, and crocodiles.

Luis often searched for the fossils of ancient birds, such as *Neuquenornis*. This drawing shows what the bird might have looked like.

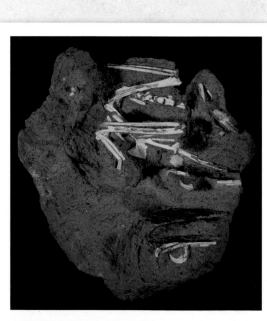

Fossils of *Neuquenornis*

Now, in November of 1997, Luis was back in Patagonia. He was leading a new expedition in a desert-like area near a **volcano** called Auca Mahuida (OW-kuh *mah*-HWEE-duh). His team's goal was to find the remains of ancient birds. Once the team got there, they found something very different but just as exciting.

Luis's team was made up of scientists and students from both the United States and Argentina.

Auca Mahuida is an extinct volcano. This kind of volcano probably will not erupt again.

A Big Surprise

It was the second day of the team's expedition. Within five minutes they came upon a sight no fossil hunter had ever seen before.

The ground was covered with ancient eggshells. In some places, Luis and the others couldn't walk without stepping on them. The more the fossil hunters looked around, the more eggs they saw. There were probably thousands of them. Many appeared to be unbroken.

This is how the eggshells looked lying on the ground.

These were not bird eggs, however. Luis could see that as soon as he picked up a curved piece of shell. It was dark gray and covered with tiny holes and bumps. These were dinosaur eggs.

Most of the shells had a rough, bumpy surface.

The area covered with eggs and eggshells stretched for a few miles in each direction. It turned out to be the largest dinosaur **nesting site** ever found.

Who Laid the Eggs?

What kind of dinosaur had laid the eggs? Luis asked himself this question right away. As he looked carefully at one of the fossils, he had some ideas about the answer.

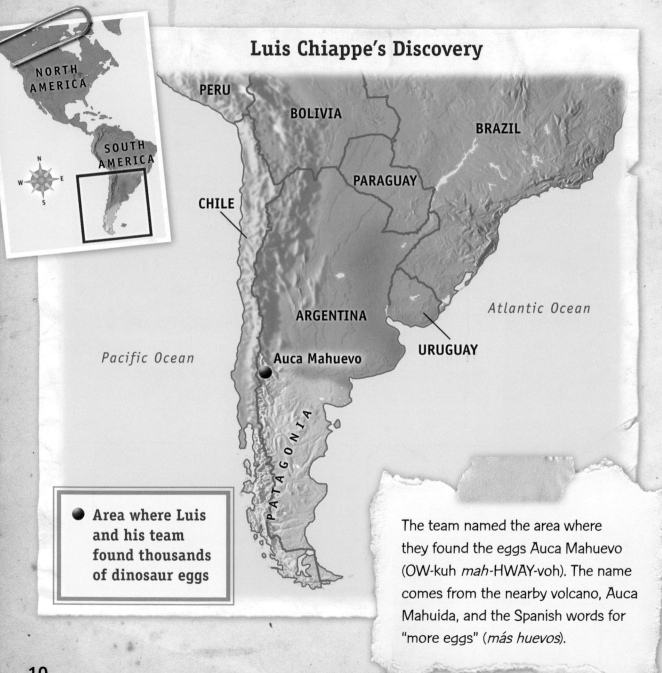

Luis Chiappe's Discovery

NORTH AMERICA

SOUTH AMERICA

PERU

BOLIVIA

BRAZIL

PARAGUAY

CHILE

ARGENTINA

URUGUAY

Auca Mahuevo

Atlantic Ocean

Pacific Ocean

PATAGONIA

● Area where Luis and his team found thousands of dinosaur eggs

The team named the area where they found the eggs Auca Mahuevo (OW-kuh mah-HWAY-voh). The name comes from the nearby volcano, Auca Mahuida, and the Spanish words for "more eggs" (más huevos).

An unbroken egg was between five and six inches (12.7–15.2 cm) across. It was just larger than a softball. Luis knew that dinosaur eggs like this had been found in many parts of the world. Due to their large size, scientists thought the eggs had been laid by dinosaurs from a group called sauropods (SOR-uh-*podz*). This group included the largest animals ever to walk the earth.

The team put a hammer next to a broken egg to show its size.

Plant-Eating Giants

Sauropods were giant plant-eating dinosaurs. They walked on four thick, elephant-like legs. They had small heads, long necks, and long tails.

Apatosaurus (uh-*pat*-uh-SOR-uhss) is one well-known sauropod. It lived in North America and grew to be 75 feet (23 m) long. *Diplodocus* (dih-PLOD-uh-*kuhss*) is another well-known member of the group. It grew to a length of 90 feet (27 m) and also lived in North America.

Sauropods were tall enough to eat from trees.

Sauropods shook the earth in South America, too. In Patagonia, the most common were the titanosaurs (tye-TAN-uh-*sorz*). This group of sauropods included *Argentinosaurus* (*ar*-jen-*tee*-nuh-SOR-uhss). At 120 feet (36.5 m) long, it is the largest dinosaur ever discovered.

Argentinosaurus

Saltasaurus

Several titanosaurs, including one called *Saltasaurus* (*salt*-uh-SOR-uhss), were covered with an **armor** of bony plates.

A herd of titanosaurs

Searching for Tiny Skeletons

Scientists had always guessed that eggs like the ones at Auca Mahuevo belonged to sauropods. So far there was no real proof, however. Luis knew that there was only one way to be sure. He and his team had to find the skeleton of an unhatched baby dinosaur inside an egg.

This photograph shows one of the few dinosaur skeletons that have been found inside an egg. The skeleton belongs to an oviraptorid, which is a small parrot-headed, meat-eating dinosaur. This fossil was found in Mongolia in 1993.

Everyone knew that finding this kind of skeleton wouldn't be easy. Unhatched dinosaurs are extremely rare. Their bones are tiny and **fragile**.

Yet the team had plenty of eggs to look at. They were eager to get started—and they soon found something startling.

The team at Auca Mahuevo started looking at thousands of eggs, one by one.

Scientists have discovered the bones of hundreds of different kinds of adult dinosaurs. However, they have discovered the bones of only about ten different kinds of unhatched baby dinosaurs.

15

Finding Skin and Bones

To everyone's surprise, the team's next discovery wasn't a tiny skeleton. It was something even rarer.

One team member showed Luis a piece of bumpy, rock-like material. It had been inside an egg. Could this be fossil skin from an unhatched baby? If so, it would be the first of its kind ever found. At first Luis wasn't sure. To be certain, the team would have to turn up more.

An egg containing skin from an unhatched baby dinosaur

A close-up view of baby dinosaur skin

Within days, Luis found more fossil skin. The team also found small brown leg bones inside an egg. The fossil hunters now had both skin and bones from unhatched baby dinosaurs. Yet they still had plenty of work ahead of them.

Baby dinosaur bones were found inside this egg.

In 1997, scientists had fossils of the skin of several different kinds of adult dinosaurs. No fossil skin from an unhatched baby dinosaur had ever been found, however.

Back from the Badlands

Over the next two weeks, Luis and his team collected many more eggs. Then they got the eggs ready for trips to two different labs—one in the United States and one in Argentina. **Preparators** would clean the fossils there so that they could be studied.

The fossil hunters were sorry to leave Patagonia, but they were also excited. Soon they might know what kind of dinosaur had laid the eggs.

After digging up clusters of eggs, the team covered them in plaster to protect them.

A preparator cleaning eggs

The news everyone was waiting for came early in January of 1998. The preparators in the United States had found skull bones and teeth inside one of the eggs. They could now say that these were probably the bones of a tiny titanosaur.

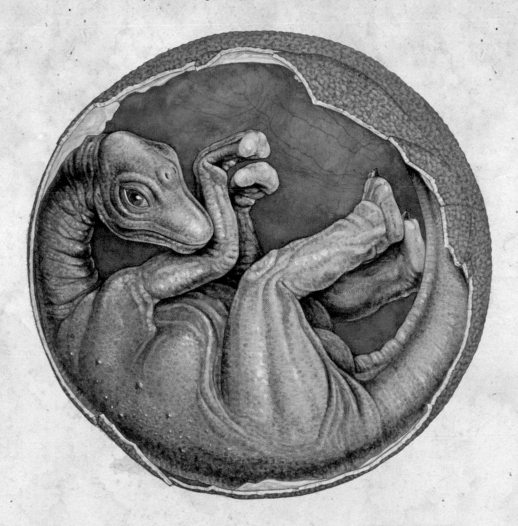

The bones inside the egg helped an artist create this drawing of an unhatched titanosaur.

The unhatched dinosaur's teeth were shaped like tiny pegs. They were an important clue about the dinosaur's **identity**.

Making Headlines

In November of 1998, the American Museum of Natural History held a **news conference**. Dozens of reporters showed up to ask Luis and other museum scientists questions about the fossil eggs.

Some of the questions were surprising. The reporters wanted to know if the scientists would now be able to grow living dinosaurs—just like in the movie *Jurassic Park*. Luis and the others explained that the chances were not good. The idea of growing dinosaurs from fossils was based on **fiction**, not fact.

Other questions interested the scientists much more. For example, what was life like for the titanosaurs that had laid the eggs and for the tiny babies inside?

In *Jurassic Park,* many different kinds of dinosaurs are brought back to life after millions of years.

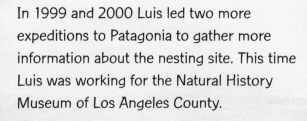

In 1999 and 2000 Luis led two more expeditions to Patagonia to gather more information about the nesting site. This time Luis was working for the Natural History Museum of Los Angeles County.

Life in the Nest

During the 1997 expedition, Luis had begun to form a picture in his mind of how the titanosaurs had lived. During his two trips back in 1999 and 2000, he and his team collected information that helped him fill in more of that picture.

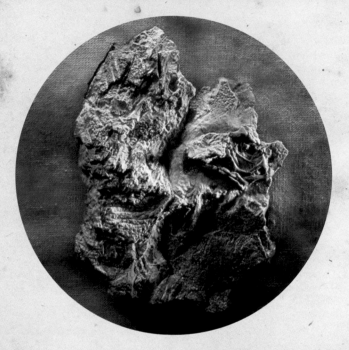

During the follow-up expeditions, Luis and his team found six eggs, each with a complete skull inside, like the one in this photograph. These tiny skeletons offered more proof that the eggs were laid by titanosaurs.

Based on the size of the bones that were found inside the eggs, Luis thinks that the titanosaurs would have grown to be 40 to 50 feet (12 to 15 m) long.

Luis could now imagine a muddy, open area near a river. The earth shakes as hundreds of females make their way there. Each one digs a nest in the mud and lays between 15 and 40 eggs. Then she covers it with leaves or twigs and goes off.

When the babies hatch, they are slightly more than a foot (30–40 cm) long. They will grow very fast for the next 20 years—until they become earth-shaking giants themselves.

Some dinosaurs probably took care of their babies in the nest. However, fossils show that the titanosaur mothers probably left the nesting site before their eggs hatched. This model of titanosaur nests was displayed at the Natural History Museum of Los Angeles County.

Death in the Nest

Luis now had an idea of how the adult titanosaurs had lived. Yet what huge **disaster** had kept the thousands of eggs from hatching?

All the evidence led Luis and his team of researchers to one conclusion. The dinosaurs had dug their nests on a **floodplain**. Heavy rains fell. The river overflowed and flooded the land, covering the nesting site with a huge blanket of mud. The unhatched baby dinosaurs died inside their eggs.

From Unhatched Baby Titanosaurs to Fossils

1 Unhatched baby titanosaurs are growing inside the eggs.

2 The babies are killed when a flood hits. Layers of sand and mud cover the eggs.

The flood was deadly for the tiny titanosaurs. Yet it was a lucky event for the fossil hunters. The mud that buried the nests also helped to **preserve** them for millions of years.

3 Millions of years go by. Most of the tiny bodies inside the eggs are crushed or destroyed by mud. A few, however, survive in the form of patches of skin and fossil bones, such as this skull.

In order to become a fossil, a dead animal must be buried quickly. The mud or sand that covers it keeps the animal from rotting away within days or weeks.

More Surprising Discoveries

Since discovering the titanosaur eggs, Luis Chiappe has continued to travel the world in search of fossils. Many of his expeditions take him to Asia. The fossils of strange, feathered dinosaurs are being unearthed there.

Sinornithosaurus **is one of the feathered dinosaurs that Luis has studied. This drawing shows what it might have looked like.**

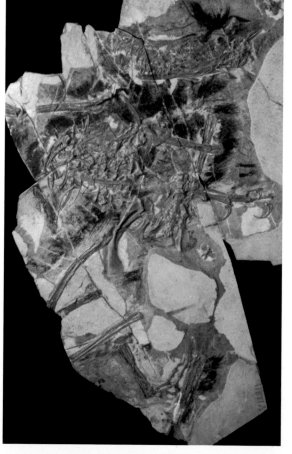

Fossils from
Sinornithosaurus

Luis has also made some exciting discoveries closer to home. Between 2003 and 2006, he and a team of fossil hunters made a series of trips to the badlands of Montana. There, they unearthed one of the most complete *Tyrannosaurus rex* skeletons ever found. While digging up the huge bones, the team also dug up something unexpected. They found the fragile remains of ancient birds—the kind of fossils Luis had been looking for a few years before in the badlands of Patagonia!

Luis uncovering the tooth of a *T. rex*

Luis's team named the *T. rex* "Thomas" after the brother of the man who discovered the bones.

A Trip Back in Time:
Who Lived with the Titanosaurs?

Dinosaurs lived on Earth for around 150 million years. Scientists divide the time in which the dinosaurs lived into three periods—the Triassic period (250 to 205 million years ago), the Jurassic period (205 to 145 million years ago), and the Cretaceous period (145 to 65 million years ago).

The titanosaurs that Luis Chiappe found inside fossil eggs lived near the end of the Cretaceous period. Here are three dinosaurs that lived at the same time and in the same places as the titanosaurs.

Carnotaurus

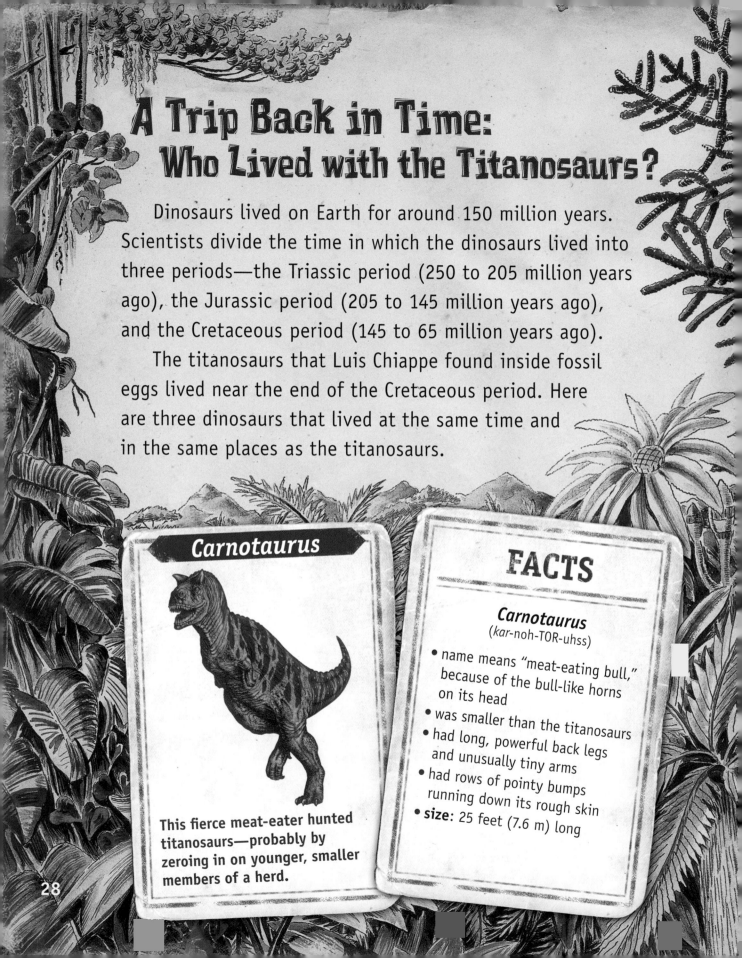

This fierce meat-eater hunted titanosaurs—probably by zeroing in on younger, smaller members of a herd.

FACTS

Carnotaurus
(kar-noh-TOR-uhss)

- name means "meat-eating bull," because of the bull-like horns on its head
- was smaller than the titanosaurs
- had long, powerful back legs and unusually tiny arms
- had rows of pointy bumps running down its rough skin
- **size:** 25 feet (7.6 m) long

Aucasaurus

This smaller relative of *Carnotaurus* was discovered by Luis's team during their 1999 expedition. Like *Carnotaurus*, it preyed on the titanosaurs.

FACTS

Aucasaurus
(*ow-kuh-SOR-uhss*)

- named after Auca Mahuevo, the place where it was discovered
- had small horns on its head
- had razor-sharp claws on its powerful legs
- **size:** 20 feet (6 m) long

Alvarezsaurus

This meat-eater lived side-by-side with the titanosaurs. Yet it was much too small to hunt them. Instead, it used its powerful thumbs to tear apart tree bark and eat the bugs that it found.

FACTS

Alvarezsaurus
(*al-vuh-rez-SOR-uhss*)

- named after Don Gregorio Alvarez, a writer who studied and wrote about Patagonia
- had a long tail
- had short arms
- had long legs and could probably run fast
- **size:** 4 feet (1.2 m) long

Glossary

ancient (AYN-shunt)
very old

armor (AR-mur)
a protective covering

badlands (BAD-landz)
an area with rocks that have
been sculpted into unusual
shapes by harsh wind and rain

disaster (duh-ZASS-tur)
an event that causes terrible
destruction

expeditions (*ek*-spuh-DISH-uhnz)
long trips taken for a specific
reason, such as exploring

fiction (FIK-shuhn)
a story that has characters and
events that are made up

floodplain (FLUHD-plane)
a flat area of land along a
stream or river that water
overflows onto from time to
time

fossils (FOSS-uhlz)
what is left of plants or
animals that lived long ago

fragile (FRAJ-il)
easily broken

identity (eye-DEN-ti-tee)
who someone is or what kind
something is

nesting site (NEST-ing SITE)
a place where animals come to
build nests and lay their eggs

news conference
(NOOZ KON-fur-*uhnss*)
a gathering where reporters ask
questions of people who have
important information to share

paleontologist
(*pale*-ee-uhn-TOL-uh-jist)
a scientist who learns about
ancient life by studying fossils

preparators (pri-PAIR-uh-turz)
people whose job is to prepare
and sometimes help find fossils
for study and display

preserve (pri-ZURV)
to protect

volcano (vol-KAY-noh)
an opening in the earth's
surface from which melted rock
or ash can shoot out

Bibliography

Chiappe, Luis M. *Dinosaur Embryos: Unscrambling the Past in Patagonia.* National Geographic 194, no. 6 (1998).

Chiappe, Luis M., and Lowell Dingus. *Walking on Eggs: The Astonishing Discovery of Thousands of Dinosaur Eggs in the Badlands of Patagonia.* New York: Scribner (2001).

Dinosaur Planet: Alpha's Egg (DVD). Discovery Communications, Inc., (2003).

Norell, Mark, Lowell Dingus, and Eugene Gaffney. *Discovering Dinosaurs: Evolution, Extinction, and the Lessons of Prehistory.* Berkeley, CA: University of California Press (2000).

Read More

Dingus, Lowell, and Luis Chiappe. *The Tiniest Giants: Discovering Dinosaur Eggs.* New York: Doubleday (1999).

Horner, John R., and James Gorman. *Maia: A Dinosaur Grows Up.* Philadelphia, PA: Running Press (1987).

Norell, Mark A., and Lowell Dingus. *A Nest of Dinosaurs: The Story of Oviraptor.* New York: Doubleday (1999).

Learn More Online

Visit these Web sites to learn more about Luis Chiappe and titanosaurs:

www.amnh.org/exhibitions/expeditions/dinosaur/patagonia/

www.infoquest.org/discoveries/discoveries.htm

www.nhm.org/tiniestgiants/index.html

Index

About the Author

Natalie Lunis has written more than two dozen
science and nature books for children. She hunts
for fossils at the American Museum of Natural
History in New York City.